Contents

Overview

From its land to its people, Canada is a diverse country. This diversity lends itself to a range of industries. Major industries in Canada include agriculture, energy, fishing, forestry, mining, and **manufacturing**. Each of these industries require people with various skills. As a result, Canadians can work in almost any field they like without leaving the country. People from other countries view Canada as a land of opportunity as well. Many come to Canada to find work, to create businesses, or to otherwise contribute to the economic landscape.

Canada's industries have global impact. The country's natural resources are shipped both raw and as manufactured products to many parts of the world. Sometimes, they are sold to other countries. On other occasions, they are sent for humanitarian

Agriculture

Agriculture, or farming, is an industry that uses the land to grow crops and raise animals for food and other products. Canadian crops include grains, such as wheat, barley, and canola, as well as fruits and vegetables. Cattle, sheep, and swine are just some of the animals raised on Canada's farms.

Energy

Energy provides the electricity that lights rooms, the gas that makes cars and trucks run, and the oil that heats buildings. It comes from natural resources such as water, natural gas, petroleum, coal, and uranium. Due to the abundance of these resources, Canada is a world leader in energy production.

Fishing

With 202,080 kilometres of coastline, Canada has access to more fish and shellfish than most other countries. Salmon, cod, and sole are just some of the fish caught off Canada's coasts. Shellfish caught in Canada's waters include lobster and shrimp. Fish farms, in which fish are raised and harvested like farm animals, also contribute to the fishing industry in Canada.

CANADIAN INDUSTRIES

MINING

Sheelagh Matthews

Weigl

www.weigl.com

Published by Weigl Educational Publishers Limited
6325 – 10 Street SE
Calgary, Alberta, Canada
T2H 2Z9
Web site: www.weigl.ca
Copyright ©2007 WEIGL EDUCATIONAL PUBLISHERS LIMITED

Library and Archives Canada Cataloguing in Publication

Matthews, Sheelagh

   Mining / Sheelagh Matthews.
(Canadian industries)
Includes index.
ISBN 1-55388-230-X (bound)
ISBN 1-55388-231-8 (pbk.)
   1. Mineral industries--Canada--Juvenile literature. 2. Mineral industries--
Economic aspects--Canada--Juvenile literature. 3. Mineral industries--Canada--
History--Juvenile literature. I. Title. II. Series: Canadian industries (Calgary, Alta.)

HD9506.C22M28 2007   j338.20971   C2006-902501-0

Printed in Canada
1 2 3 4 5 6 7 8 9 0   10 09 08 07 06

All of the internet URLs given in the book were valid at the time of publication. However, due to the dynamic nature of the internet, some addresses may have changed, or sites may have ceased to exist since publication. While the author and publisher regret any inconvenience this may cause readers, no responsibility for any such changes can be accepted by either the author or the publisher.

Project Coordinator: Heather Kissock
Designer: Warren Clark

We gratefully acknowledge the financial support of the Government of Canada through the Book Publishing Industry Development Program (BPIDP) for our publishing activities.

Credits: Every reasonable effort has been made to trace ownership and to obtain permission to reprint copyright material. The publishers would be pleased to have any errors or omissions brought to their attention so that they may be corrected in subsequent printings.
Logan, Sir Edmond (1978–1875), c. 1860. Photographer unknown. Toronto Public Library (Toronto Reference Library): page 17; **Courtesy of Nuna Logistics Limited**: page 33.

purposes, in order to help countries that have an urgent need for materials. Canadian products are known worldwide for their quality. In order to maintain and improve this quality, Canadians are constantly developing and implementing new technologies and methods, all the while keeping an eye on the impact these technologies have on people and the environment.

Canadians can work in almost any field they like without leaving the country.

Forestry

Forests cover about 40 percent of Canada's land surface, and approximately 245 million hectares of these forests are timber-productive. This means that the trees in these areas can be used to manufacture other products. Spruce, pine, cedar, and fir are all timber-productive trees found in Canada's forests.

Mining

Minerals of all kinds are found deep inside Canada's land. These minerals have a range of uses. Once it is mined from the ground, Canada's zinc is used in sunscreen. Its sand and gravel are used to build houses and roads. Its gold and diamonds are used to make jewelry. Other minerals mined in Canada include copper, potash, and nickel.

Manufacturing

Canada uses its natural resources to create a variety of products. At pulp and paper mills, trees are used to make paper. Nickel is used to create stainless steel for eating utensils. Besides sunscreen, zinc is also used to create the galvanized steel used in the construction of buildings, aircraft parts, and telecommunication equipment.

Profile

Sir William Logan (1798–1875)

Sir William Logan founded the Geological Survey of Canada (GSC) in 1842 and served as its first director for 27 years. The GSC was the first Canadian scientific organization, and has since made a major contribution to the country's economic growth.

Logan and his staff provided a sound preliminary knowledge of the geology and mineral resources of Upper and Lower Canada. This knowledge laid the foundation for later mineral discoveries and more elaborate studies.

At the GSC, Logan's main objectives were regional mapping and the evaluation of potential mineral deposits. The importance of both field and laboratory studies, still form the basis of the present-day GSC. Through his published reports and exhibits, Logan was also responsible for bringing Canada's mineral potential to the notice of the outside world.

Logan was born in Montreal in 1798. He studied briefly in Edinburgh, Scotland before his uncle sent him to Swansea in Wales to oversee an investment in a new smelting process. As a result,

Logan developed an interest in mineralogy and in solving geological problems. His lack of formal education in geology was typical of the times, and he gradually became an acknowledged expert on copper and coal.

In 1843, he started work on the coal fields of Nova Scotia and New Brunswick and later that year began exploration of the Gaspé Peninsula. His reports in following years covered the

> **The importance of both field and laboratory studies, still form the basis of the present-day GSC.**

geology of Ottawa, the Lake Superior region, and the geology of Quebec, especially the Eastern Townships and the North Shore, the north shore of Lake Huron, the gold-bearing gravels of the Chaudiere region and the southeastern part of the Canadian Shield.

The work was not detailed by today's standards, but it

■ People had been using coal as energy for many years when Sir William Logan discovered how coal is created from plant fossils deep within the earth.

was accurate and thorough. Annual reports of activities were published which led to discoveries and the investment of capital for development.

Logan was knighted by Queen Victoria in 1856 and awarded the Order of the Legion of Honour by the French emperor. During his career he received 22 medals in all.

Reprinted with permission from the Canadian Mining Hall of Fame website at: www.halloffame.mining.ca

Careers in Mining

There are all kinds of job opportunities in mining for men and women alike. Some jobs, such as a miner's job, are directly involved with the operation of a mine. Others help the mining industry indirectly by refining, transporting, and selling valuable ores brought to the surface. Mining is a many-faceted industry requiring workers with different skills and education levels.

Exploration Geologist

Duties: Explore for mineral deposits, help plan mines

Education: Bachelor or master's degree in science, with a specialization in geology

Interests: Rocks, adventure, outdoors, travel, mathematics, chemistry

Exploration geologists are needed to determine where mines should be built, if at all. They spend days and weeks searching for rocks, checking rock samples, and re-checking geological data in the search for earth-bound treasures. When working "in the field," exploration geologists spend most of their time outdoors collecting rocks and data on the area. They work long hours in the field, sometimes 12 to 14 hours a day. When in the office, they analyze the information collected in the field. Due to the scientific nature of the work, exploration geologists are always learning something new.

Exploration geologists work in the field collecting and studying rock samples.

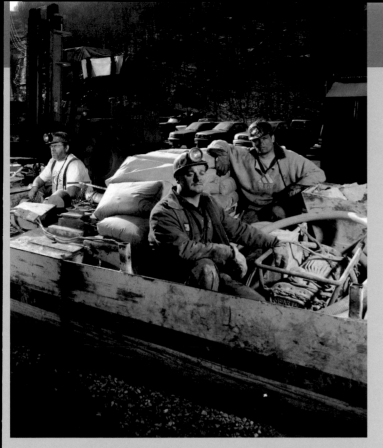

Miners extract various materials from the ground, including coal, gold, and diamonds.

Miner

Duties: Drilling, hauling and blasting rock, moving and sorting supplies, workplace safety

Education: High school education with mining training program

Interests: Rock, operating equipment, handling explosives, physical work

Miners, the core workforce of the industry, carry out various tasks in underground or open-pit mines, such as operating drilling and hauling equipment and handling explosives and blasting. They load, move, sort, and pile materials and supplies, and keep underground work areas and equipment clean. Miners also keep the mine safe by reinforcing the mine walls and by clearing any ore or coal spills. Miners can progress to higher level jobs with experience and training.

Environmental Scientist

Duties: Make sure the mine is operating in an environmentally-sensitive way

Education: Bachelor or master's degree in science, with a specialization in biology, **ecology**, or **environmental science**

Interests: Biology, outdoors, wilderness, wildlife, mathematics

Environmental scientists are needed to help plan for environmental protection before, during, and after mine operation. Before mining projects are approved for construction, companies must show how the mine will not have lasting negative effect on the land, air, and water in the area. Over the last 10 years, mining companies have started creating executive positions to manage their environmental responsibilities. These scientists must keep up with all the new technological advancements for mine-site **reclamation**.

Some environmental scientists study water to make sure it has not been polluted by mining operations.

Facing the Issues

The world looks to Canada for mineral resources. These resources help other countries stock factories and produce goods, thus providing the people of these countries with jobs and a better lifestyle. As a result, the demand for Canada's mineral riches, especially metals, is very hight. Canada exports almost 80 percent of its mineral production to the rest of the world every year.

In 2004, almost 52 percent of all mineral production in Canada was from metals. High demand for metals helps keeps prices up, but high demand also contributes to a decreasing supply of metals. Known as a country of vast resources, Canada's metal **reserves** are now in the process of depleting. Depletion of metal resources is the biggest challenge facing the Canadian mining industry today. For the first time in history, in 2004 Canada imported more metals than it exported. It is possible that lead production in Canada will cease within five years.

This depletion of resources is a happening due to the principles of supply and demand. Canada has resources that other countries need, but do not have. Countries such as China, with its growing population of 1.3 billion people, are becoming more industrialized every day. As these countries become more

In 2004, almost 52 percent of all mineral production in Canada was from metals.

In the mid-1800s, Canada began commercially producing copper at Bruce, Ontario. Copper has been mined coast-to-coast in Canada, from British Columbia to Newfoundland.

It takes 300 years for an aluminum can to decompose in the garbage.

industrialized, they are building more roads and factories, driving more cars, and needing more fuel and energy. These countries look to Canada for many of the raw materials needed to build their businesses. In order to keep up with the high demand, Canada must find ways to maintain its supply of mineral resources.

One way to combat Canada's shortage of metal resources is to recycle those resources already in the marketplace, such as iron ore and metals from old cars, gold from computer chips, lead from batteries, and copper from wiring. Recycling and re-using are very important strategies for any non-renewable material, including Canada's mineral resources.

Canada must also continue the search for new mineral resources. Unless new discoveries are made, metals mined in Canada may be seriously depleted by 2014. This could lead to a loss of jobs caused by closing down smelters and refineries. Transportation incomes would also decrease, as minerals account for more than half of Canada's rail and port volumes. Without exploration and new finds, Canada stands to lose its global position as a leader in minerals production.

Debate

Canada's declining supply of metal minerals comes at a time of high demand. What should Canada do? Develop better mining methods? Develop more mines? Develop a better recycling system?

YES By developing better mining methods, more ore can be extracted from existing mines at a faster rate.

By exploring for and developing more mines, Canada can better keep up with world demand.

By developing a better recycling system, Canada will not need to find as many new mines. There will be less demand for minerals, allowing Canada more time to find alternative materials to replace these minerals before they are all gone.

NO By developing better mining methods, this only depletes Canada's supply of minerals faster.

By exploring for and developing more mines, Canada's supply of minerals is only depleted faster. Minerals are non-renewable resources—once they are gone, they are gone.

By developing a better recycling system, Canada's mineral resources will have more than one life. When people no longer have a need for new things, manufacturing will drop. This could lead to factory closures and job losses.

 Abandoned mines are an economic drain. They are also harmful to the environment.

About 10,000 orphaned or abandoned mine sites have been identified in Canada. Many of these sites are hazardous to both people and the environment. If the owner of a hazardous orphaned or abandoned mine is not found, provincial and federal governments become responsible for the site. Today, new mines must have plans to put closed mines back to their original condition, or as close to original condition as possible. This is called mine reclamation. Technological advancements provide ways to lessen the mining industry's "footprint" on the environment.

Any job where people could get trapped underground has potential danger. Canada's mining history includes serious disasters claiming the lives of many men. The Hillcrest Mine, a coal mine in Alberta's Crowsnest Pass, is the site of Canada's worst mining disaster. On June 9, 1914, just before the start of World War I, 189 of the 235 miners on shift died as the result of an explosion in a mine shaft 1,600 feet underground. Methane gas and coal dust, probably ignited by a spark, caused the explosion. The Hillcrest cemetery is now a historical site.

Canada's Worst Coal Mining Disasters

189 dead—Hillcrest Mine Disaster, Crowsnest Pass, Alberta, 1914
75 dead—Springhill Mine Disaster, Glace Bay, Nova Scotia, 1958
26 dead—Westray Mine Disaster, Pictou County, Nova Scotia, 1992

Helping Others

Canadians in the mining industry are helping to make the world a better place. Although the world is rich with mineral resources, not all parts of the world are rich. People in developing countries often live in dire poverty even though they may work in mines that make a great deal of money. The Prospectors and Developers Association of Canada (PDAC) wanted to turn this situation around. Since mining is a way to generate economic wealth in a developing country, PDAC decided to ask the World Bank to get involved. In 2003, PDAC asked the World Bank Group to use its influence to direct investments to countries where mines treated workers fairly. Large investments for mines are almost always required because mines are very expensive to operate. It was hoped this would encourage mine owners and governments to share the wealth created by mines and pay workers fair wages. In 2004, the World Bank Group agreed. In the future, World Bank Group mining investments will focus more on the needs of poor people and environmentally and socially sustainable development.

Extreme poverty is forcing people to mine small amounts of gold to help feed their families.

Not all countries use the same technology or techniques for mining.

36

Sometimes, miners in the Philippines must handle gold that has been mixed with mercury.

Mining in many countries is not as safe as in Canada. There are almost 15 million people in more than 50 countries involved in primitive, low-cost, small-scale, unhealthy, and environmentally damaging gold mining activities. Extreme poverty is forcing people to mine small amounts of gold to help feed their families. Millions of mine workers in Sudan, Indonesia, and Brazil use mercury to access the gold, with little or no concern for their health or the environment. Mercury is a toxic substance and should be used with great care. The University of British Columbia is working on the Global Mercury Project to lessen the effects of mercury used in mining. The goal of the project is to develop inexpensive mining technologies that poverty-stricken miners can afford to use. Then the Global Mercury Project will go about the task of teaching miners how to use these new technologies. The Global Mercury Project also tries to get tighter restrictions on mercury exports from Canada to reduce this problem.

Mining and Modern Society

Thanks to mining, people around the world enjoy its many benefits.

- Wages to pay for food, shelter, and education

- Materials to create needed household items

- Materials to build roads, schools, and houses

- Materials to build cars, trains, ships, and planes

- Materials to supply factories, science labs, and mints (currency)

Looking to the Future

Future global demand for Canada's mineral resources, especially metals, will be driven by China and, to a lesser extent, India. If Canada wants to remain a leader in mineral production, it must find more resources to meet these needs. Developing better recycling technologies, especially for metals, will also help Canada stay competitive in the minerals market. New frontiers for Canada's mining industry might also include deep-ocean mining or mining in outer space.

Space age mining is no longer the stuff of science fiction or fantasy.

Treasures from the Sea

Ocean explorers have found jets and springs of very hot water rising from cracks in the ocean floors. These streams of hot water sometimes carry various minerals in solution which, when cooled, later turns into mud and crusts. Armed with this new information, scientists might be able to find future sources of mineral deposits that can be recovered from the ocean.

Scientists have also discovered potato-shaped **nodules** of metals, including manganese, copper, cobalt, and nickel, on the ocean floor. When these nodules are too far from land, ocean miners may consider using offshore recovery methods similar to the oil and gas industry.

Magnesium, bromine, and salt are three minerals already mined from the sea. These minerals are dissolved in the seawater and mined when found in high concentrations.

Scientists believe that deep-sea mining may be possible in the near future. Gold-mining companies are already collecting samples from the ocean floor.

Space Age Exploration

Space age mining is no longer the stuff of science fiction or fantasy. In fact, exploration for minerals in space has been taking place since *Apollo 11* first landed a man on the Moon. That early lunar landing mission included gathering 20 kilograms of lunar material to bring back to Earth for analysis. More recently, NASA's robotic rovers "*Spirit*" and "*Opportunity*" have been sent to Mars to collect rock samples and take photographs. In 2004, the rovers confirmed that at least one place on Mars had a wet and possibly habitable environment long ago. Even though they are far away, the Moon, Mars, and other planets might become sources of important mineral deposits for mankind to use in the future.

Studies of rock and mineral samples from Mars may one day help scientists understand how mining could be successfully performed on Mars.

Insider Viewpoint

What does the future hold for Canadian mining? Take a look at what one person working in the industry thinks.

"Twenty years ago, most mining companies didn't want to hear about [undersea mining]. They thought it was too difficult. But now some are seeing that it's a lot easier to go down through a couple of thousand metres of water than through a couple of thousands metres of rock."

Dr. Steven Scott, University of Toronto

Timeline of Mining Events

40,000 BC

Copper is traded among Aboriginals in the Lake Superior region.

200 BC - AD 200

Silver is traded in the Cobalt, Ontario area.

998

Vikings mine bog iron at L'Anse aux Meadows, Newfoundland.

1577

Martin Frobisher mines 200 tonnes of rock on Baffin Island.

1604

Samuel de Champlain notices copper and iron deposits in the New World.

1639

A coal mine opens at Grand Lake, near Bay of Fundy, New Brunswick, to supply coal to Boston. It is likely the first coal mine in North America.

1643

The first shipment of coal from New Brunswick to New England is reported.

1737

The first iron smelter in Canada opens at Trois Rivieres, Quebec.

1809

The first sailing of John Molsons' *Accommodation* occurs, marking the introduction of steam navigation on the St. Lawrence River.

1823

Gold is discovered in Quebec.

1842

The Geological Survey of Canada is established.

1852

Gold discovered is in British Columbia.

1860

Gold discovered is in Nova Scotia.

1862
The Cariboo Gold Rush occurs in British Columbia.

1866
Gold is discovered in Ontario.

1870
Coal mining begins in Lethbridge, Alberta.

1883
Copper and nickel are discovered near Sudbury, Ontario.

1896
The Klondike Gold Rush occurs in the Yukon.

1900s
Iron deposits are found in northern Ontario.

1903
Silver is discovered in Cobalt, Ontario, sparking a "silver rush."

1907
The Canada Department of Mines is established.

1909
The Geodetic Survey is established, continuing today as Natural Resources Canada.

1911
Coal mining begins at Drumheller, Alberta.

1914
The Hillcrest Mine Disaster occurs at Crowsnest Pass, Alberta.

1950
Uranium is discovered in Saskatchewan.

1958
The Springhill Mine Disaster occurs at Glace Bay, Nova Scotia.

1991
The first major discovery of diamonds in Canada occurs in the Northwest Territories.

1992
The Westray Mine Disaster occurs in Pictou County, Nova Scotia.

1998
The Ekati Mine, in the Northwest Territories, is the first diamond mine to open in Canada.

2003
Canada's second diamond mine, the Diavik Mine, opens in the Northwest Territories.